The Spaces We Inhabit

Colin Read / Reade Collins

© 2020

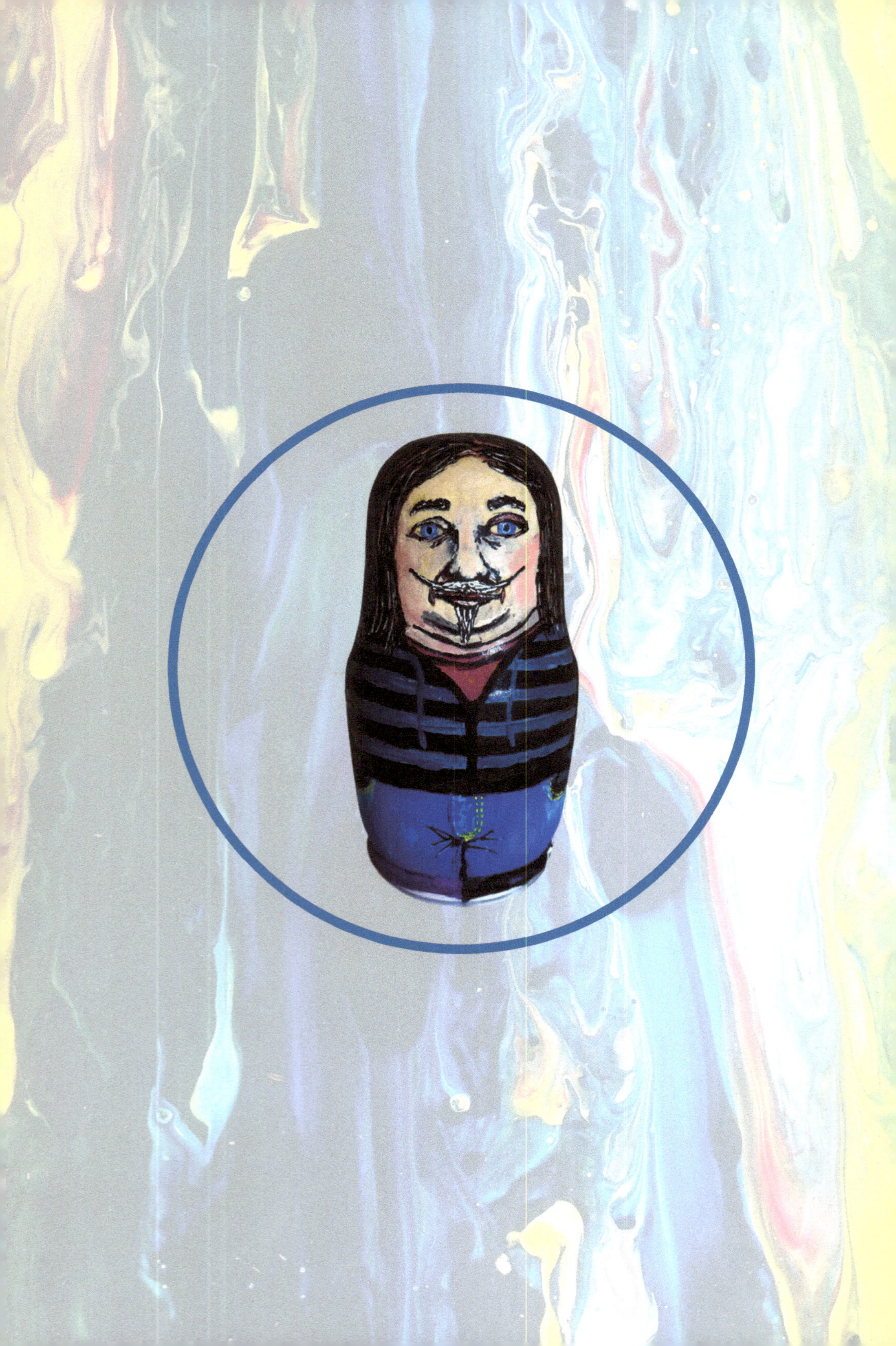

Contents

The Spaces We Inhabit – Parts 1 and 2

Part 1: Topographic Gradients

There is beauty
In the hidden gradients
Formed by the topography of life
Variations in the attitudes
Define the colours of each moment
And pixel by pixel
We scan the secret abstractions
And subtle shadings
Of the spaces we inhabit

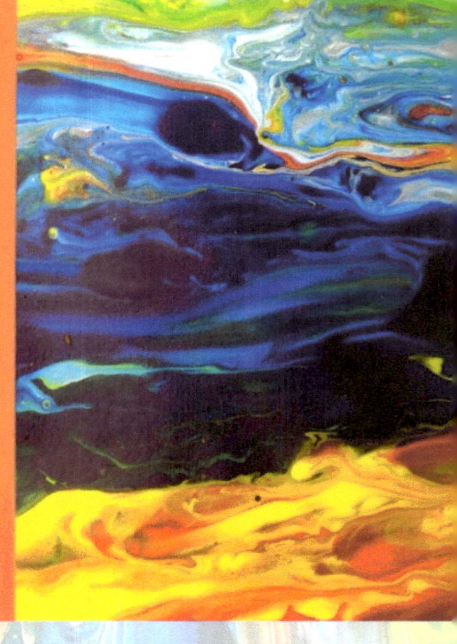

Part 2: Ghosts of Our History

We are the ghosts of our history
A narrative we reconstruct
From fleeting glimpses
Of our remembered selves
Ephemeral, we believe ourselves
To have substance
As our atoms fade and fall away
Along all the future pathways
Of the spaces we inhabit

Colonial Shahada

This is our home
We are bound to this land
Pana; earth; desert; loam;
Boulder; rock; sand.

In dreaming truths;
In ancient word -
Our being, infused;
Our nascence, conferred.

Traders; trepangers;
Chinese sailors;
Ujung Pandangers;
High seas "travaillers" —

They came to our shores,
Exchanging their wares,
Respecting our laws,
To fish bêche-de-mer.

A little Dutch dove made land in our north —
One hundred and sixty-four years before Cook —
No gentle feathered softness held in its breast
Harsh arrogance and self-conferred worth
Gave rise to conflict we could no longer brook
Our retribution gave it flight to the west.

Belonging, connected and melded. For two teraseconds
We spoke, we sang this country – our synergistic history.
Unknown to us, the notion of Terra Australis Incognita beckoned
And Terra Aquilinos Notum crossed oceans; to endow inflicted misery.

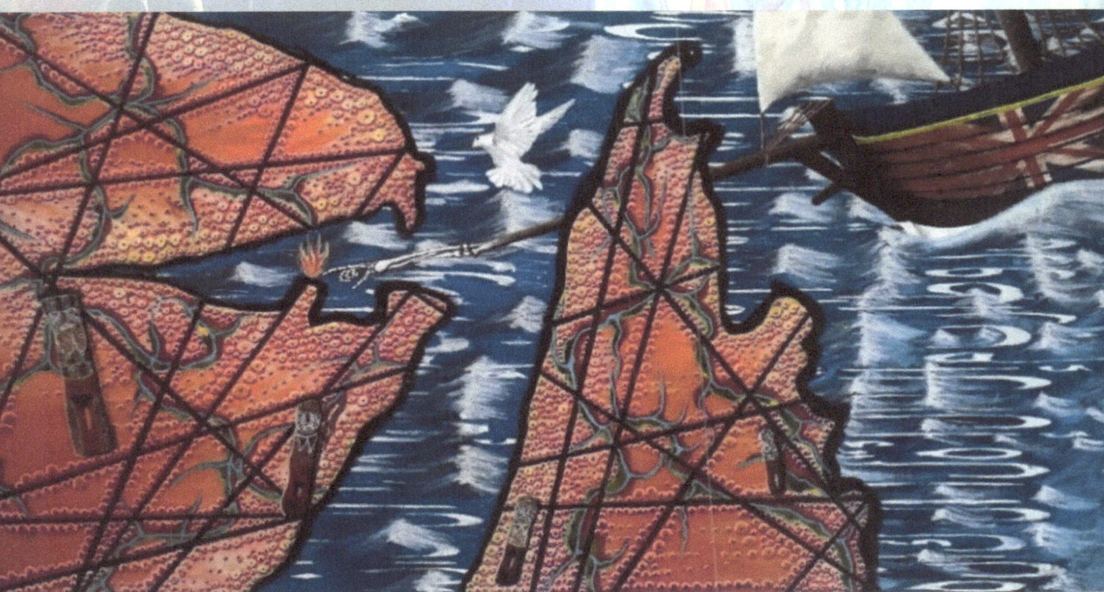

It was then that you came
Then you laid claim
In defiance of our presence,
Our ways of the land
Terra Nullius was enacted.

We traversed our living country in joyous lines of song
You replied with despotic dirges of vivisection
Carving up your new procurements

Comfortably blameless in the salving justifications
Of your unique Eurocentric
Esoteric
Legalese
Of fence lines and rule,
Titles and deeds.

You bestowed upon us the status of fauna;
A fauna to be controlled and overcome
In proclaiming the Terra as Nullius
We had no recourse
When you took what was ours.
For in that simple and swift decree
We became less than
The dingo, the snake,
The emu, the roo;
Your cattle, your sheep,
Your bullock, your mule.
As beasts to be tamed;
As vermin to be exterminated;
As bugs to be stamped out;
As vexations to be eradicated.

Your self-righteous belief
In your mode of civilisation
Surreptitiously taught us
To succumb to yourself
Fulfilling prophesies
Of a natural attrition.

Encouraged by
Introduced diseases,

Instituted bounties;
Endorsed in
Self-justified,
Arrogant blind-eyed,
Whispered then denied
Reified
Genocide;
Engrossed in,
Obsessed with,
Breeding out the black –
Retribution for not happily adopting,
Or adapting to,
Your singular vision
Of how humans
    (Especially those who do not share
    Your history
    Your commerce
    Your dogma
    [Your Shahada]
    Your greed
    Your colour),
In your sanctimonious opinion,
Should, naturally, desire to live

"You have no choice.
You must evolve and mutate.
Deny your voice."
Is your hubristic mandate,

"For there is no other god than the Empire
   And colonialism is its only profit"

Invite Blindness (To Lead Us)

I picture myself
As blind,
(But I don't believe I really am).

I see
Through the eyes
Of a
White,
Cisgender,
Heterosexual,
Baby booming,
Middle class,
WASP-ish
Male.

I do not wish to
Make assumptions
And
Interpret others
From within
This profiling's
Hardwired
Limitations.
After all
We are probably
Nothing more
Than a
Temporary, ephemeral, finite mass
Of atoms –
Particles of

Minimal import
In the seemingly
Interminable and boundless
History and dimensionality
Of this
Universe

(This is not my curse alone).

We are all challenged –
By differences
And otherness –
To invite
Blindness
To lead us
Into gentle curiosity
And celebration of all
Uniqueness –
Into hungered learning,
And humbled openness,
To hear the stories
Of all
Individualities.

When I was
A teenager
I was
Consumed
By the wonder
Of the belief
That the most
Powerful

And incomprehensible;
Potent,
Yet inexplicable force
In this universe was
Love –

Abstract and concrete;
Intangible and palpable;
Desired and elusive…

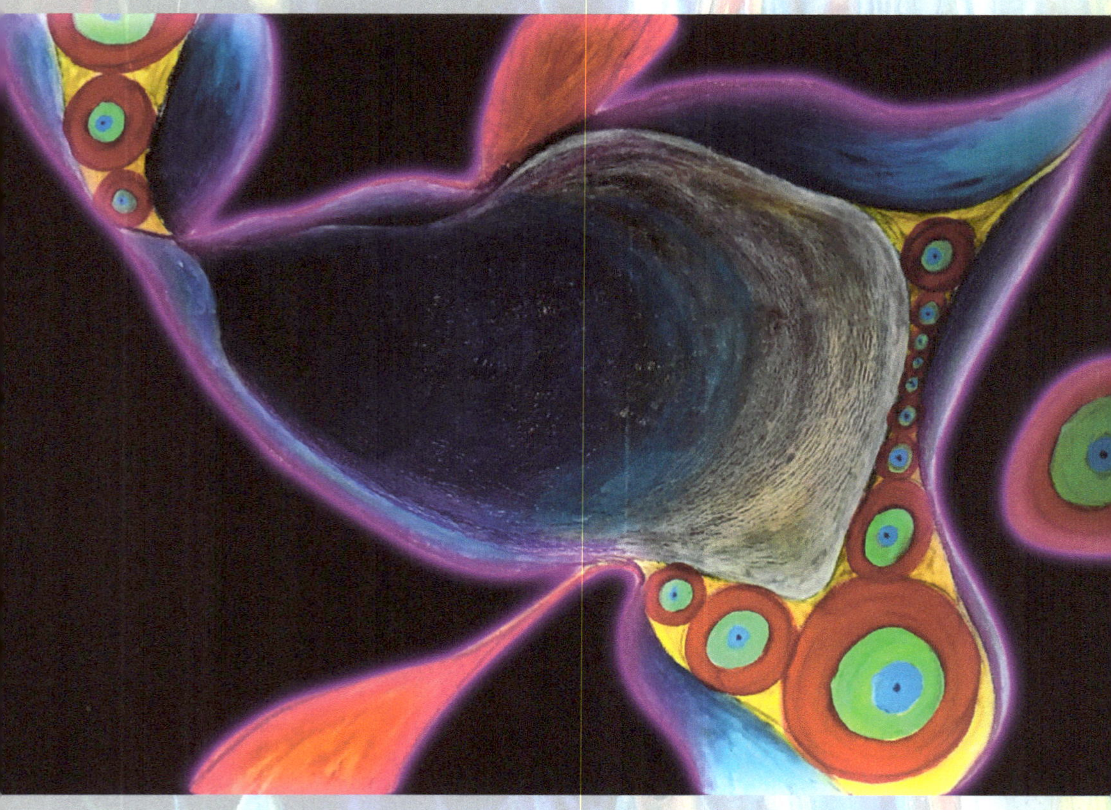

Somewhere.
Somehow.
Sometimes…

I still believe
It is only love
(Embodied in commitment
To surrender)
That will render me
Blind enough
To have no need
To ever look back
Again.

I still believe
It is only love

Screaming Motor Mower Saturday

Screaming motor mower Saturday
Scraping fingernails
Down
The blackboard of my tranquillity
I was chalking up
The totality
Of the calming interplay
Gifted by
This Sabbath day –
Joyous magnanimity –
When all my peace
Was ripped away –
Shrieking mower on a Saturday

Is the volume
Of your blaring klaxon
Inversely proportional
To the level
Of your caring action?
When it comes to
The bleeding of my ears
Your situational compassion
Is put aside –
It disappears.
Motor mower
Bullied to levels
Beyond eleven…
I am driven to distraction.

As I start to realise
Tomorrow is Sunday
My heightened pulse
Begins to lower;
I might yet relax
For that one day –
Ah… my rapid heart
Beats somewhat slower;
(I only hope and pray
That you do not start
Your fucking blower!)

You

The first time that you saw me
Curled up as a ball
Rocking, trembling, weeping,
Afraid that I would fall

From the precipice of reason
Into the slathering maw
Of my inner purgatory –
Anhedonia's mort d'amour,

Did you know I was in terror
From the mewling caterwaul
Of the dread beasts deep within me
Their relentless, hateful call?

I had deadened my emotions –
There was emptiness inside –
I had built a wall around me,
Invited death to walk beside –

To become my soul companion –
I suppressed all joy of living,
Blockading every entry,
No receiving and no giving.

But then you came and held me
And gently took my hand,
Your love completely felled me,
And now I understand

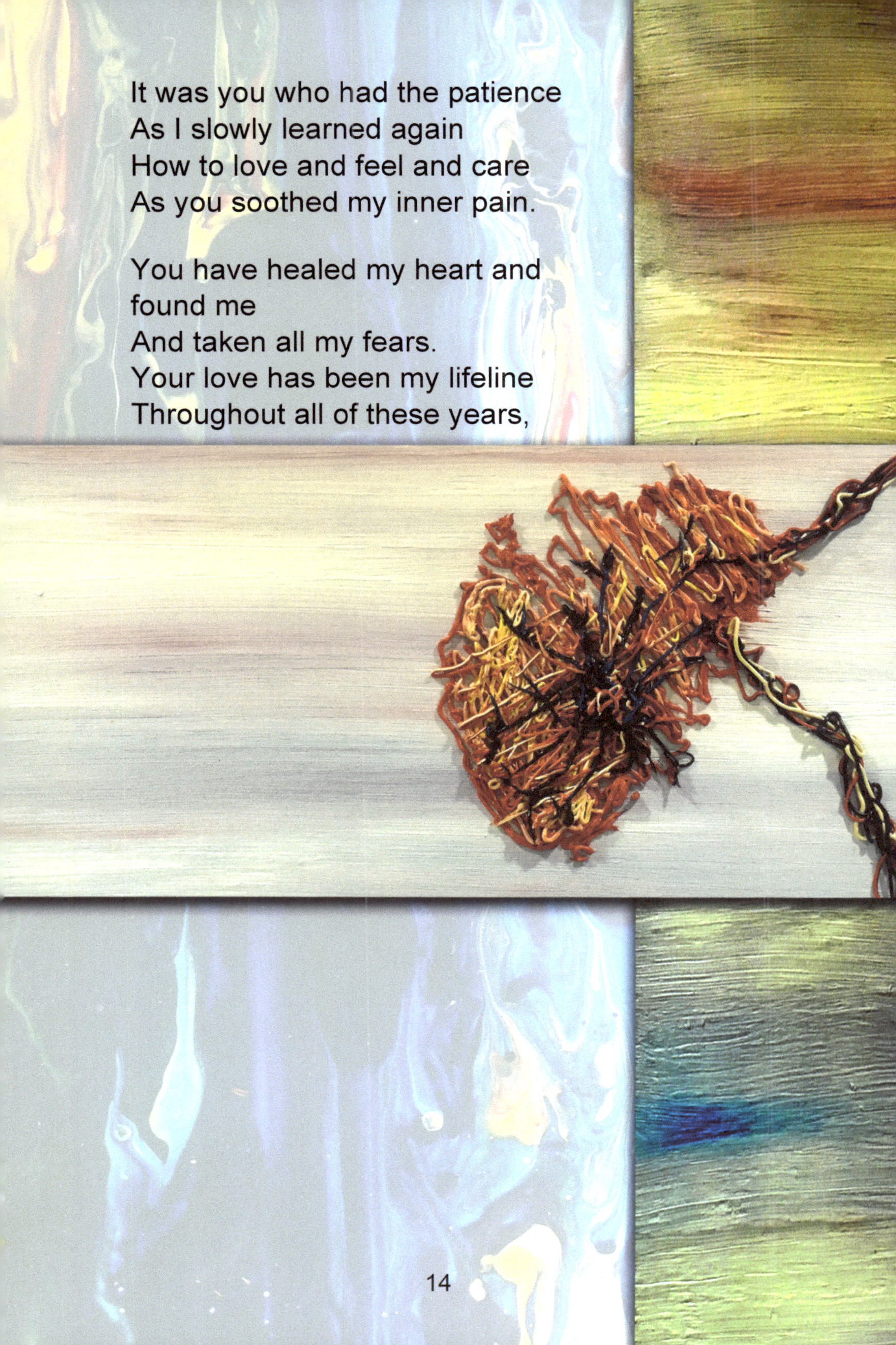
It was you who had the patience
As I slowly learned again
How to love and feel and care
As you soothed my inner pain.

You have healed my heart and
found me
And taken all my fears.
Your love has been my lifeline
Throughout all of these years,

Puppet

Abandoned sock
        Alone
        Your partner gone
        Into the black hole –
        The nexus between
        This world as a pair
        And the universe of lost
        And discarded
        Objects
        Companionless
        I will take you
        Anthropomorphise you
        With
Button eyes
        And woollen sewn eyebrows
        Looking with all
        Semblance of sight
        But never seeing
        Appearing to engage
        But without connection
        To any internal
        Occipital interpretation
        Inside only
        Thumb and digits
        To form your
Muffled mouthpiece
        As the vet performs
        Bovine palpitation
        So too,
        I shall perform

Palpitation on you
You will have
No voice,
No thoughts,
No words:
My ventriloquatee;
My
Fingered footman
Prodded and poked
Dependant
Volitionless minion
Your animation
Is contrived by me.
Your self-will
Is my capricious whimsy
My fickle predestination.
I am the handler
And you, the
Handler's muff.

Pig in a Python

I am part
Of that generation
Defined by
Economists
Historians and
Anthropologists alike
As
"a pig moving through a python".

We are fat
Replete with the consequences
Of our initial
Boonful blessings
And the subsequent
Inevitable indolence
Of our collateral greed.

We have selfishly
And parsimoniously
Held tight to ourselves
The gift
The hope
The future –
Erected bollards
Across the prospects
Of the freeways
On which we freely sped
To our expected
Destinations.

It is our
"Love of money
Which [is become]
The root
Of all [our] evil".

We have built
Upon the sandy foundations
Of our economic
Rationalism
Refusing to bequeath
The benefits
We took for granted
Our privilege we read as rights
Creating an existential certainty
That we would simply
Be able to walk away
Whilst those
Coming after
Would be crushed
In the ineluctable
Collapse
(A predestination we had surely
Ordained in our fatal actions)

And I am
Enraged
By our callous arrogance

And I am
Overwhelmed
With tears and weeping

And I am
Desolated by

The schisms in our amity

The ignorance and arrogance
Of our foresight and hindsight.

The regulation of our compassion

The politicalising of our succour

The monetisation of our humanity

Dogs' Eggs (Wrapped in Plastic)

She always knew
What came first –
The chicken or the egg?
Of course –
It was the hen.
After all
It was the hen
She had first seen
Squeezing an egg
Out of its butt
Which led to her earliest
Cross-nomenclature
When, soon after,
She witnesses a dog
Performing
A very similar feat.
"Dogs' eggs!" She had exclaimed

Unlike hens' eggs
These were usually
Longer
And browner
And softer
And often found
Discarded on footpaths,
Nature strips,
And front lawns.
No brooding here
Abandoned

To slowly disintegrate
Slough off in the rain
Or harden in the sun
To a dusty, chalky, white

And so it was that
Over the years of
Crap encrusted heels
And shit shod soles
It became socially
Decreed de rigueur
That all pooch and pup
Pedestrians should be:
 • Restricted by leash;
 • Chaperoned by human;
 • Pursued by plastic bag
   To be used for the sole
   Purpose of:
      i.   Scooping up:
      ii. Confining, and;
      iii. Disposing of
           Any miscreant
           Sole shit shodding,
           Heel crap encrusting
           Dogs' eggs

In time
She came to fear
The visions
That would suddenly invade
Her thoughts –

The seemingly inevitable
Chomolunginas,
Chhongoris, and
Kangchenjungas –
A complete orogenic belt
Of polyethylene encased dogs' eggs,
Of turds in plastic
A formidable
Mountain climbing legacy
For her children
And her children's children.

In retrospect
Maybe their original
Un-intervened
Innate
Ability to
Decompose and compost
Into the humus of
This world's
Repurposing decay
May well have been
The better option
And worth
A few soiled soles.

A "Blip" is in Retrospect

"I have seen the long-term trend, and the current warming is a small blip on the historical scale..."
- An argument presented by climate change denial apologists

He walked the woodland road
Along the path that took the shoulder
Shoulder to shoulder
With the forest
And the corrugated gravel
Physical onomatopoeia
To the gravel
Of his voice
"Too many of these shit sticks!"
He growled through the cumulonimbus
Roiling with a minor thunder
From his lungs
And flicked the barely smouldering
Short end tailings
With the conviction that
Only his suckling drags
Had maintained its ember.

As it hit the track taken
Unconscious dogma
That life support
Was now immutably denied
Doused contemplation of
An enduring multiverse

Three things
Does a fire need to burn:
    1. Fuel
        (The underbrush and dried grass edging
        the path gently stroked by)
    2. Oxygen
        (The susurrating breeze, rejuvenating)
    3. Heat
        (The embers' waning "étincelle de vie")

When he reached his destination
He looked back
And saw
A maelstrom firestorm
Raised up
And all around
Was razed and erased
To ash

Suck the Eggs

Suck the eggs
And frack the dregs
Dredge the ball
From wall to wall
Like a mindless
Vegetable
Given time the
Crust will fall

Bifurcation
Degradation
Global nation
Desiccation
Warming oceans
Set in motion
Disharmonic
And atonic
Deathly chronic
Earth dystonic

Plastic seas
And CCDs
Disembowel
The honey pot
Disavowal
The final shot
At rationale
For moneys got

Archimedes' Ocean

A man runs naked down the city street
Water dripping from his shoe-less feet
He cries, "Eureka! The answer is complete!
Displacement is the volume's balance sheet!"

The secret of the bath is finally won
The water's cryptic knowledge is undone
And manifest, flows forth as waters run
The hydrologic cycle has begun

Five oceans are the oceans' hydrosphere
Where ever water flows, the fact is clear
From bath to sea, from lake to stream and weir
The universal law does yet adhere

And so we "drop by drop" into the sea
From butts to straws, from ships to NSP,
We defecate, acidify and pee
As struggling island nations pay the fee

The Great Pacific Garbage Patch is fed
The North Pacific Gyre is its bed
And blanketed with nurdles, as they spread,
Eurythenes plasticus has been bred

Warming, melting, rising, poisoned, lost
The balance of the deep blue, double crossed
The biologic pump will bear the cost
As the stewards manufacture holocaust

She Just Says, "Moo!" || She Farts

How do I tell you about her?

Do not anthropomorphize
Her

I suppose
Some would describe her
As a little bit
On the 'beefy' side

For me
It is always her
Doleful eyes
That talk to me
And capture me
With their deep
Inner
Sadness

Although she
Lives in the field
One perfect day to the next
And day-to-day
Twice daily
Like one of the obedient herd
She dis-engorges
The conclusion of her
Rumination

Sunrise to sunset

She does not know
That there is work being done
To synthesize
Her and her
Four stomach chambers'
Yield
Maximized through
Generations of genetics

Perhaps it is for the best
But
Where will she
And her sisters
Go
Then?

She stares at me
She chews her cud
She just says, "Moo!"
She farts

Foreverness

We fuck
Standing
In your mother's kitchen
Your arms
Your legs
Wrapped around
And I
Am holding you
Up

I remember

Through the sun-washed venetians
Down the scoria topped drive
Across the road
Past the caretaker's home
And the school's football ovals
Over the valley
To the newly subdivided fields
Where houses sprout like
Mushrooms of the urban sprawl

You whisper into my ear
Your joy
Of
Summer skirts
And no underwear

Mass, time and space
Disband all pretence…

We were invincible and enduring

The memory's emotion
Crushes me
To the point of
An equal intertwining of
Another little death
Literal and metaphysical
Lethal and malignant

And I cannot bear the loss
Of that all at once
Foreverness

Maw and Gullet

Chef de cuisine
Grounds and grinds
With mortar and pestle
Disdainful of each prescribed step
All arrogance in self-assured certainty
That this is the dish to be served
Is the dish to be served
The dish to be served
The ingredients
Morsels of bitterness
Sour and acetic
Shredded slithers of pungency
Drizzled vinegris and brakish
Mixed to glutinous paste
A porridged bolus
Mucilaginous phlegm
Slimed and tenacious

If this is
The dish to be served
It will be
The dish to be eaten
Sticked and funnelled
Into maw and gullet
Of the gull(et)ible masses

Is there nothing
Compassionate
Hopeful
Loving
A la carte?

The Fragmentationalists

The fundamental maxim
Of the fragmentationalists
Is embedded in abstractions
Of in extremis axioms
Unfathomable antics
Sequestered in semantics
Self-truths that beg defiance
From the factualness of science

And we are us to us
As they are us to them
And they are them to us
As we are them to them

Once language was important
In attempts to sublimate
Now we self-fulfil all prophesies
With talk of war and hate
The egocentric narcissist
Who only says, "I am"
Whose greed for self surpasses us
Is now the "everyman"

And we are us to us
As they are us to them
And they are them to us
As we are them to them

Rationalised economies
Nationalised theonomies
Political protectionism
Profiteering acquisition
Trickling down as micturition
On the dis-em-manumissioned
Drowned in rising imposition
Of fractious factitious perdition

And we are us to us
As they are us to them
And they are them to us
As we are them to them

And the fragmentationalists declare

This is just
Like war

    We must reframe our language –
    To gain a clear advantage
    Rephrase the lingua franca
    To justify our rancour

    To speak in words of weapons
    Our lexicon – aggression
    Pre-emptively to threaten
    Malignant Armageddon

The enemy to be opposed
Our enmity to be composed
All threats to be eliminated
All empathy exterminated

And the fragmentationalists declare

This is just,
Like war

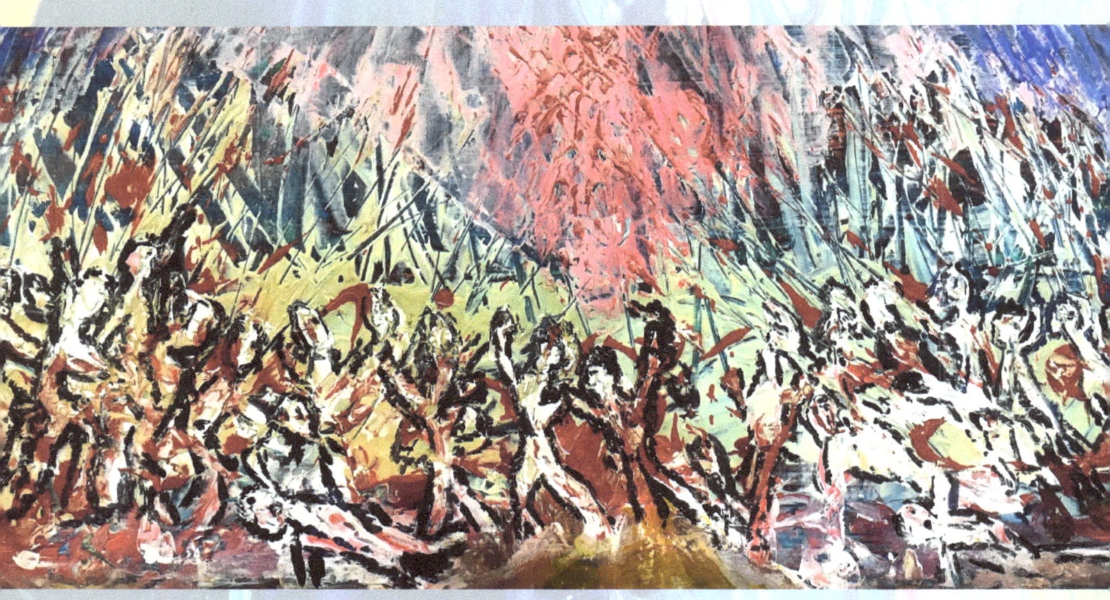

And we are us to us
As they are us to them
And they are them to us
As we are them to them

In Between the Quanta

In between the quanta
Sits the space of eternity

Our reality lies there
In the combination
Of our acknowledgement
And interpretation
Our agreement
And accord

We maintain the truth
Of our shared reality
Through our collective
Cognition
We affirm the
Generalities of existence
In the details of
Our mutual consensus

Observed
Named
The intangible
Becomes
The revealed occult
The created ex nihilo

The Enormity of my Insignificance

(I too have desired the sun)

Icarus
I too have desired
The sun
And wilfully misconstrued
The image
Built for myself
Insisting my glory
Be worshipped
In reflections
Of a broken mirror
(This is delusion
And shards will pierce
In random instances
Of life
For seven times seventy times seven hundred
Years)

I am fallen
Melted wax
Deplumes
Ocean bound
I swim to the moon
And drown
In the enormity
Of my insignificance

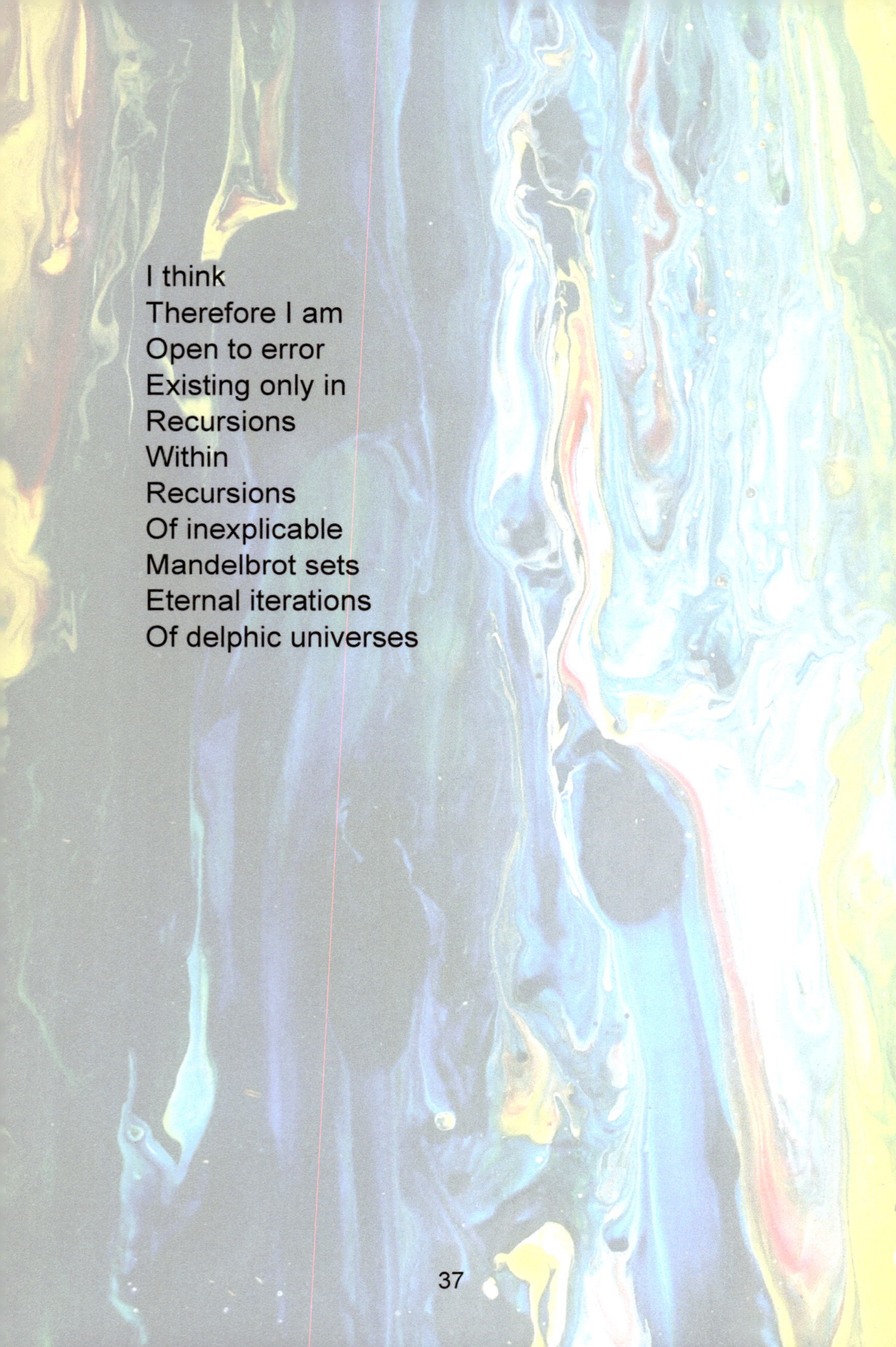

I think
Therefore I am
Open to error
Existing only in
Recursions
Within
Recursions
Of inexplicable
Mandelbrot sets
Eternal iterations
Of delphic universes

Then Yaw and Roll

There are days
When we live
In the flight path
The north wind blows
The planes fly over
From the east
Then yaw and roll
Into our boreal australis

The paths
The roads
The highways
Diese luftbahnen
Are
For now
Less travelled
The rightful of the skies
Repossess their realm
The beasts of Bird-dom
Reclaim their domain
In blissful songs sublime

At night
Our windows used to rattle
On the testing engines' seismic winds
Sleep was broken and restless

Now we can sleep
But the tumultuous nightmare roar
Of those
Tremorous cyclonic dreams
Prevail

Late spring firestorms
Endemic pandemic
Ammonium nitrate

Corymbia Citriodora (Befall the Horolation)

Down the down
Back the back
Corymbia Citriodora
Sounds the sounds
"Chacka! Chack! Chack!"
Amongst the leaves and flora

Audacious loquacious,
Antiphonal
Trichoglossus moluccanus
Volacious bodacious
Antics 'n' all
Tricksy joshes frolics charm us

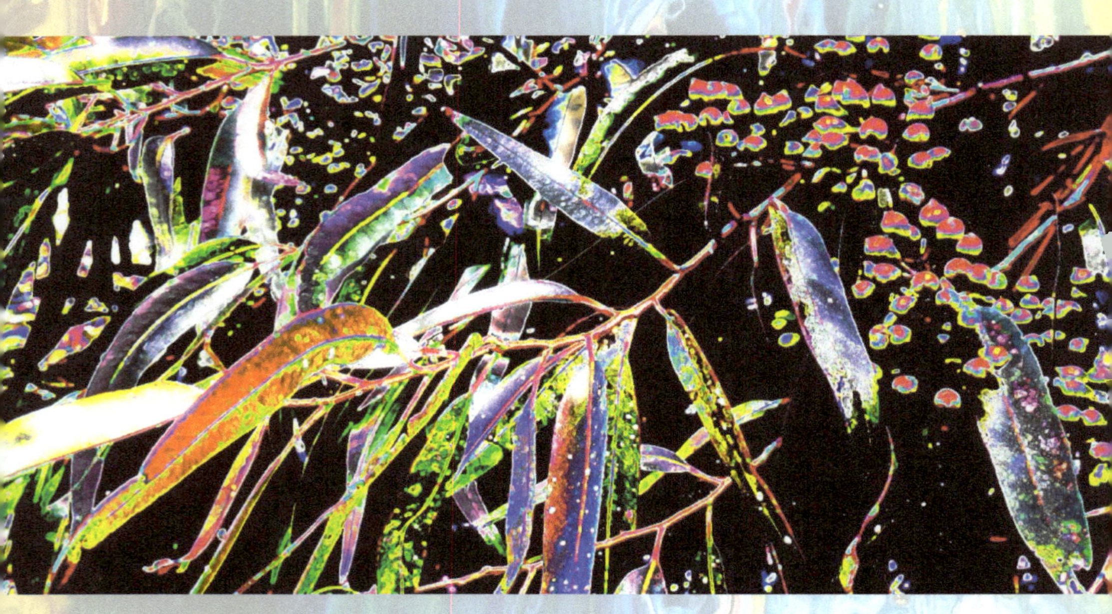

Sit and set
Breath and breathe
Citronellal perfume teases
Flicker flecks
Lambent leaves
Coccinellids' purview - breezes

Branching branches
Branch off branches
Arborescent iterations
Dancing dancers
Susurrant cantors
Ambient alliterations

Close I
Close eyes
Introspective rumination
Flows by
Grows my
Meditative contemplation

All is all in trance formation
I befall the horolation

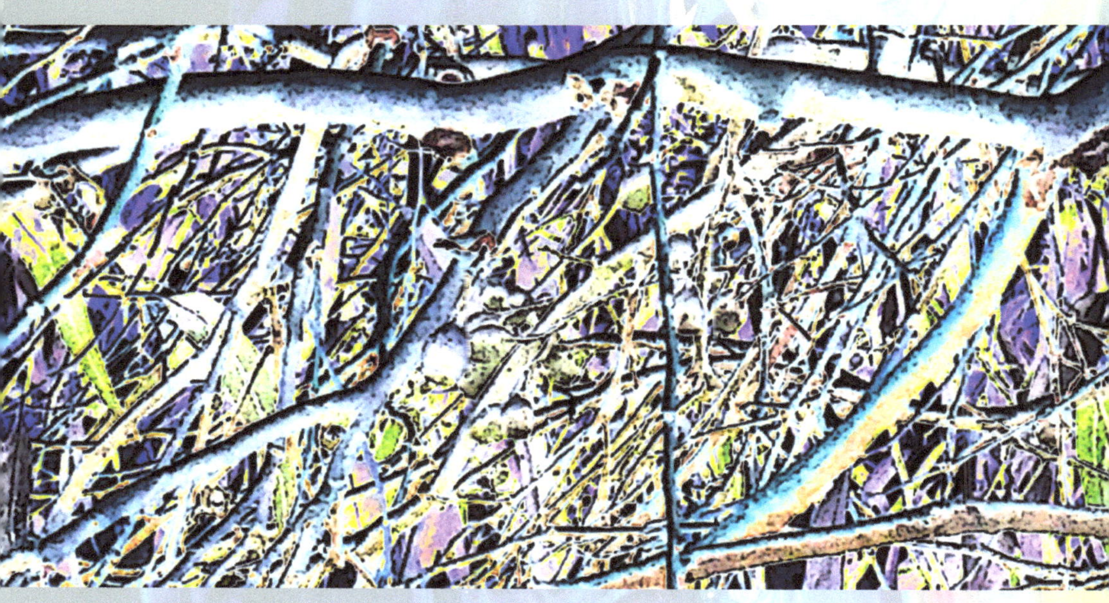

No Batteries Required

Early winter morning
(I want to say
Crepuscular
But that would likely be
Way too pretentious
[Maybe pretentious is
In itself
Way too pretentious
So please replace
Pretentious with
Wanky])

Anyway
Back to where
I was:

Still dark
I was sleeping –
Still should be –
But
A smoke alarm's
Battery is running low
And needs replacing
Predictively repetitious
Regularly prodding my stupor
With stopwatch accuracy

Beside me
She is snoring
Or at least

She is feigning sleep
Through her addled somniloquy
(Still wanky
But far more woke
Than
Sleep-talking)
And prodding
I get the message
To find the dying
Smoke alarm
And perform a
Lazurus
Pack in 9 volts of
A power packing
Power pack
And shut
The bloody thing up

Barely purposeful
Torpid
I slug and sloth
Through the house
Looking for the offender
Its guiding clockwork
"Ping!" ... "Ping!" ... "Ping!" ...
Finds me staring at the ceiling
In the room
Next to our kitchen

I am staring at the ceiling
Trying to locate a smoke alarm
That I know has

Never been there
I start believing
I am still
Crashed abed in
Nod

Weirdly the believing
Brings a clarity
That confirms
My newly founded beliefs
Incorrect

I

Re-bunk?
Re-crib?
Re-couch?

Go back to bed

"Dizz yer fixsh it?"
Is mumbled through the gaining light
I smile,
"No batteries required."
And slip into
The blanketed cocoon
Once again
While our newly resident
Bellbird
Celebrates the gum tree
In our front yard

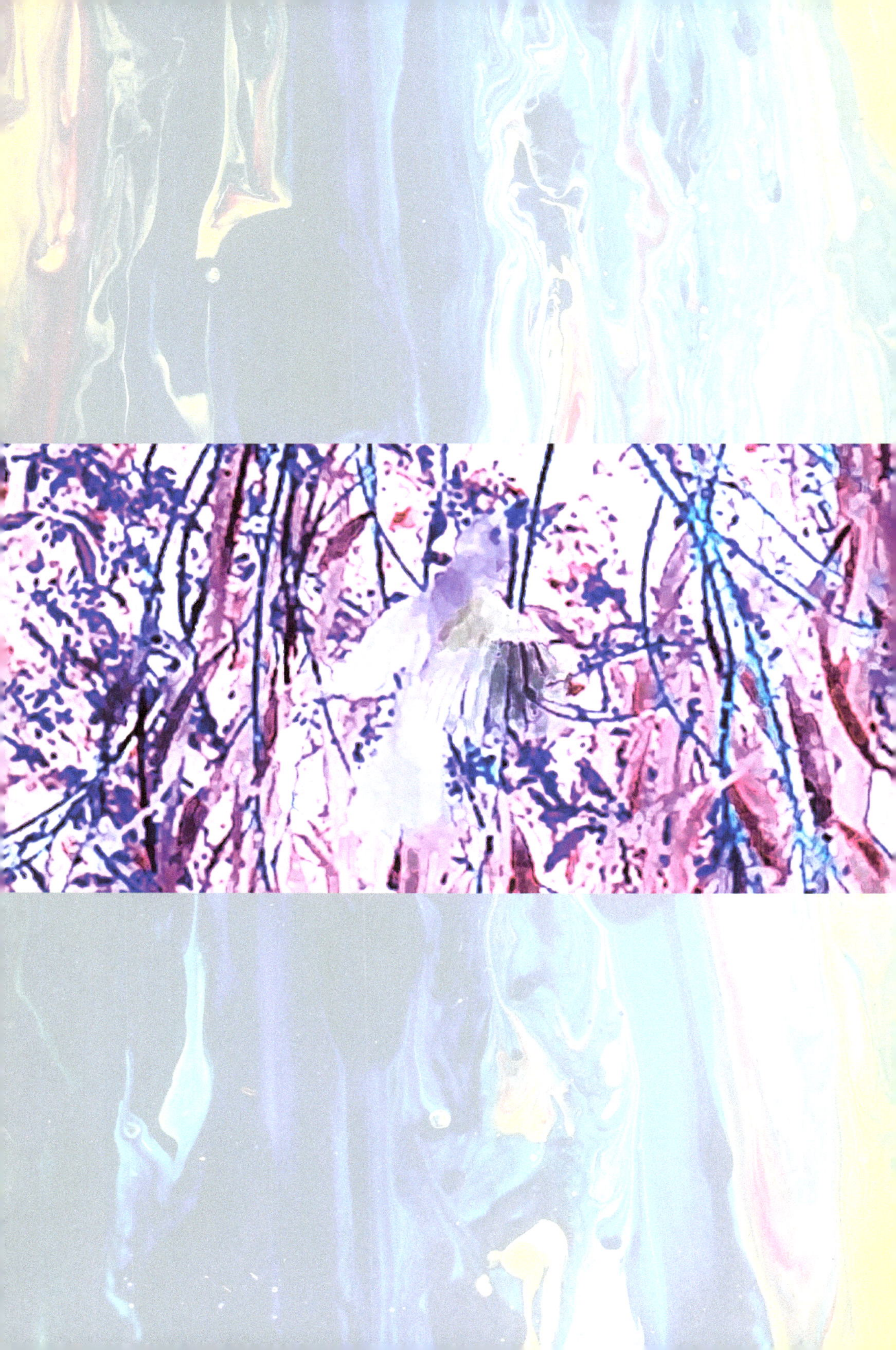

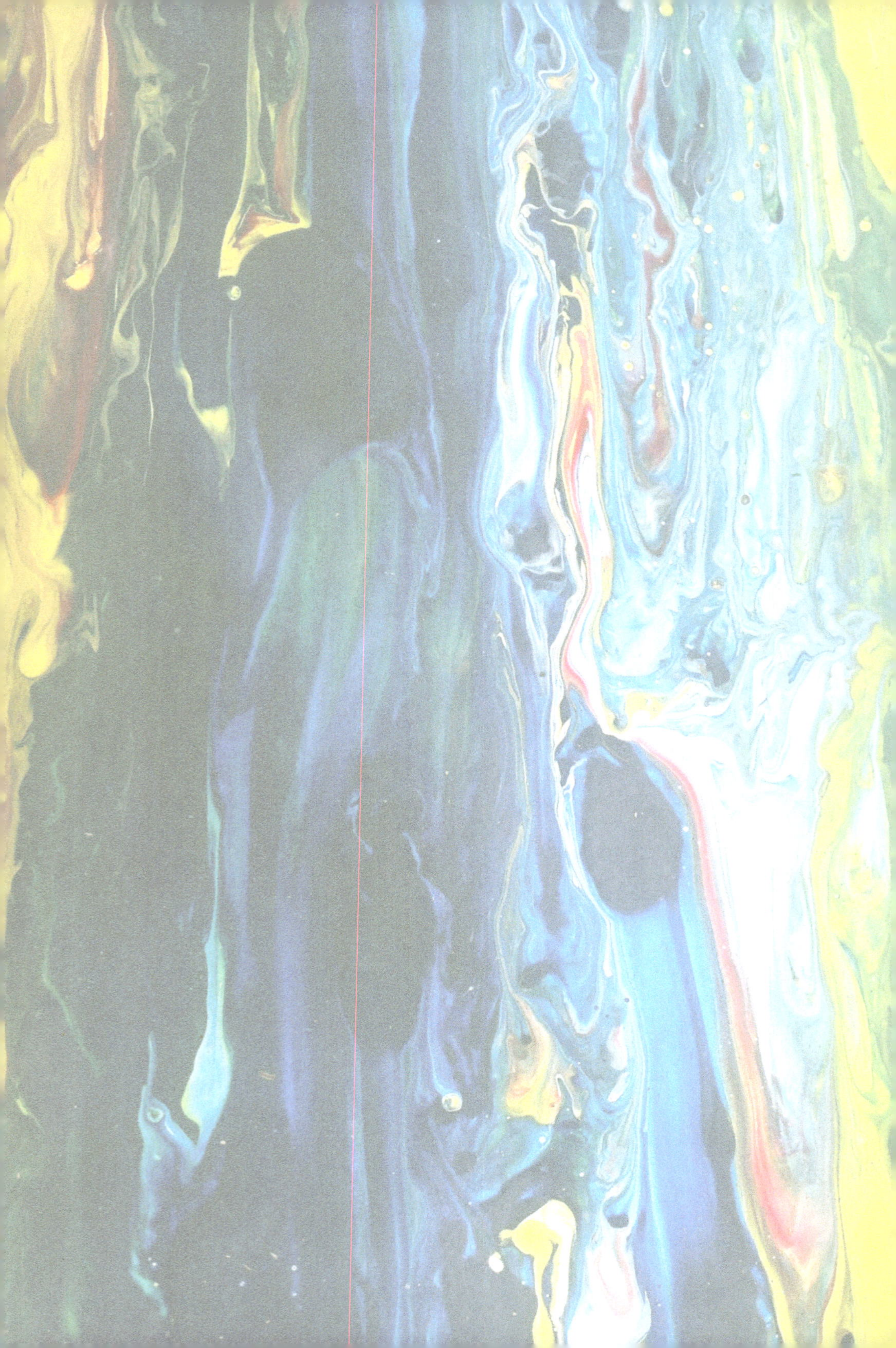